PENGUIN BOOKS

FIELD OF VISION

Stephanie Horvath's poems have appeared in *Bennington Review*, *Gulf Coast*, *Poetry Northwest*, and *Denver Quarterly*, among other journals. A former Wallace Stegner Fellow, she lives in Northern California and teaches at Stanford University.

The National Poetry Series was established in 1978 to ensure the publication of five collections of poetry annually through five participating publishers. The Series is funded annually by Amazon Literary Partnership, William Geoffrey Beattie, the Gettinger Family Foundation, Bruce Gibney, HarperCollins Publishers, the Stephen and Tabitha King Foundation, Padma Lakshmi, Lannan Foundation, Newman's Own Foundation, Anna and Olafur Olafsson, Penguin Random House, the Poetry Foundation, Amy Tan and Louis DeMattei, Amor Towles, Elise and Steven Trulaske, and the National Poetry Series Board of Directors.

THE NATIONAL POETRY SERIES
WINNERS OF THE 2025 COMPETITION

Field of Vision by Stephanie Horvath
CHOSEN BY ELISA GONZALEZ FOR PENGUIN

Low Flying Planes by Hajjar Baban
CHOSEN BY JAKE SKEETS FOR MILKWEED EDITIONS

Wildest by Kira Alexis Tucker
CHOSEN BY SIWAR MASANNAT FOR AKASHIC BOOKS

Cloud Builder by Weston Morrow
CHOSEN BY ARIANA BENSON FOR UNIVERSITY OF GEORGIA PRESS

Diary by Yi Wei
CHOSEN BY SASHA ROQUE PIMENTEL FOR BEACON PRESS

FIELD *of* VISION

Stephanie
Horvath

PENGUIN BOOKS

PENGUIN BOOKS
An imprint of Penguin Random House LLC
1745 Broadway, New York, NY 10019
penguinrandomhouse.com

Pages 63–64 constitute an extension of this copyright page.

Set in Adobe Caslon Pro
Designed by Sabrina Bowers

LIBRARY OF CONGRESS CATALOGING-IN-PUBLICATION DATA

Names: Horvath, Stephanie (Poet) author
Title: Field of vision / Stephanie Horvath.
Description: New York, NY : Penguin Books, [2026]
Identifiers: LCCN 2026008565 (print) | LCCN 2026008566 (ebook) |
ISBN 9780143139393 paperback | ISBN 9780593513484 ebook
Subjects: LCGFT: Poetry
Classification: LCC PS3608.O77735 F54 2026 (print) |
LCC PS3608.O77735 (ebook)
LC record available at https://lccn.loc.gov/2026008565
LC ebook record available at https://lccn.loc.gov/2026008566

Printed in the United States of America
1st Printing

The authorized representative in the EU for product safety and compliance is Penguin Random House Ireland, Morrison Chambers, 32 Nassau Street, Dublin D02 YH68, Ireland, https://eu-contact.penguin.ie.

"No soy como mi muñeca, que sólo se nutre
de leche de pájaro"
—ALEJANDRA PIZARNIK

("I am not like my doll, who feeds
only on bird's milk")

CONTENTS

I

II

III

IV

V

FIELD *of* VISION

I

THE RESCUE

I carry the boy from the fire

For once I'm done thinking all the time about money

I carry the boy from the fire, I'm not even thinking
about you, or work, or anything, just the boy

They put a long silver needle through a bedroom wall
to show me the coordinates where his mother is waiting
I don't mind if I have to walk forever, I'm carrying

the boy on fire. Over my shoulder, his legs that are on fire are
dangling. In the smoke I see one lone snake born slow

from an egg, gray and slinking. I carry the boy
People in crowds nearby look at us, they are pointing

There is a tall wooden cross on a hill over the highway
where deer feed on hawthorn and cherries

I carry the boy past the tall wooden cross,
past the vineyard, past the orange trees

Men I have been with have told me their nightmares,
the times that they hurt or killed others in dreams

You said you had strangled a man at the depot,
that the police were on your heels

I carry the boy from the fire
I don't cut him

I've got him over my shoulder
and I'm brushing the flames

from his body like breadcrumbs
I don't throw him

into the river

CONSTITUTIONAL

The sun goes down and the people practice piano.
You can hear it from open windows.
You can smell the onions sautéing
in corridors that used to be regular old streets.
The people have emptied out of a ship.
There are jellies beached beside the driftwood.
You see through them to the inside. Invisible
organs, clear heart, clear divide between the waves
and the mouth of the bay, which had to begin
with itself to end up this way.

FRAMEWORK

This was the first heat of spring.
That space where a sheep
dragged her stomach through the grasses.

I knew it by instinct, how to take
the pulse of an animal. If not by the heart,
then to trace out an artery close
to the hind leg, feeling for heat.

Time would of course keep moving.

The culvert's fixed place beside the river.

Your gloved hand to wrest the lamb
without protest into the field later that week.

Serene and narcotic, born already walking.

I was a child. Rehearsing my legwork and aerials
on the narrow expanse of the river beach.

A papermill smell through the air, thickening.

Sometimes you come back.
Crossing the line into New Russia Township.
   Mourning doves batting the dirt with their wings.

An average recall of washing much smaller hands in the stream.

My towel was yellow.

Things that I couldn't believe or make sense of.
The nighttime shape of it.

You imagine this all to be far
in the distance. No, it is eating the grain beside your feet.

ROAD ATLAS

In western Oregon, there are mountain orchids
that grow best where fires have been. After
the damage, fragile as tissue, they wake.

In Maine, there are lawns full of ships
sealed in plastic. There are wet streets at night,
smooth and black as the long backs of whales.

I hear the sound of water collapsing.

I see by my injuries like streetlights.

On the coast, there are skates' dried eggs
in small black cases across sand,
            you could shake them
like maracas. There is something wet
and religious all over the beach.

I am in the Dakotas, all my hazard
packed into the small car
  and prairie dogs shoot up from holes.

In small towns, the golf courses die
  from excess of money and liver.
Bad conversation, and no one remembers
the animals nearby,

they break branches with their bodies,

I was born there, the mother
would lift me slow from a sink to dry
and mountain orchids grew over the earth.

BULLFROGS

A gradual arrival. I could trace their whole
progress with my nondominant hand
and almost get bored: a neighbor's vineyard,
a roiling above in late spring, a low drone,
a bellow. Then the light of the morning.

The days continue, the clouds go on.
I have been there, in the texture of butter,
parsing the world for a certain heat.

Some women save photographs
of themselves in labor.
I wasn't one of them, but I find it
transposed sometimes onto certain things,
the plastic chair-back I hugged in the shower,
an inarticulate baritone that couldn't
possibly have come from me.

Dressed for the evening,
the eyes are distracted,
bending one arm to catch the soul
as it falls from her sleeve.

Later the look of the outside world
from a saran-wrapped window.
Searching for that bastion of light,
a smell that we both lived in.
Wearing your shirt
in the hours you're away at work.

Beneath the eave of the upholstery repair store,
waiting out rain. Liquor-mouthed, long ago.
A pain I could appreciate in abstract terms.

Wanting above all to be loved.

Abundant, heard all night from the pond.

FERAL ROCK DOVE

Most of my life, I have been a heavy stone.
One thing leaves another. The worms
their underground tunnels. The cicadas
their coats. The sadness California.

I dream of a hill without weather.
I get lost inside of its underdressed trees.
North, I miss your fitful skies, but there is a hill.
Sagebrush, desert sand, swelling organ of sea.
The corn snake its skin. The person her apartment.
Every piece of the door with its primary function:
to be this, a piece of the door. We meet once more
in a small afternoon, in a place where the rivers
have already started to freeze.

It is across her bloated chest you'll most clearly observe
the iridescent sheen. Flown over the length of the field.
Flown over incidents. A year of absence, yellow
mushrooms adjoining linoleum, flown over
the unmade bed and the wood floor: silent,
and ungrooved. Water-sensitive and nameless.

Flown over the marble Mary—acid-washed, virginal.
Mothers in snow await sleds by the base
of the *Slow Down* sign. Flown over horses in stables
who sleep standing up, over chimneys left houseless
and severed plains, over the cruelty,
and flying, still, over the sickness. Knowing
the vastness to be vastness, I sense her overtaking me.

What is a bird's ear?

I put my ear to where her ear would be.

MUD SEASON

I lived in a trailer on another woman's property
for three years. I watched her from the window.
I remember a time when I didn't need to eat as much
because I was somebody else's obsession. I knew
I'd keep existing because they were always imagining me.
I think it is my fault the woman is becoming all skin and bones
lately. She pries the stubborn witchgrass from the compost pile
and uses a mesh screen to sift rocks and roots from the soil.

Soon I will step out to help her.
It is where I left the vintage sleigh bed, the dehumidifier.
A broken station wagon with someone else's
parking permits. The placenta. As usual, I am frightened
by the subjective nature of art, what makes something
good. Another wasted spring. The leaded Victorians,
with gold-painted window frames and pastel awnings.
That ceramic concern on the face of Cybill Shepherd.
In a North Texas oil town, her unaged cheek comes
to seem the most suitable space for a tear. Is that good?

Times before you'd arrived, I could still rest
on the couch and cry, or watch a movie. "Don't you know
it's bad luck to compare hands?" one woman says
to another. Later the mute actress's face changes slowly
into the face of her nurse. Loose fists domed
over flashlight bulbs. "This is your blood," one child says
to another. Now it isn't a movie. A rat gathers tissue
and shredded paper in the boiler closet, intending to stay
the entire length of the season. The woman supplies us
with snap traps, steel wool, and six latex gloves.
For a few minutes in the shower, out of your earshot,
I try to recover from what I have seen.
Faux wood veneer over everything. The romance of necessity.

I am past it now, but soon these will be your memories.
I describe the movies out loud because that is how
they become, once more, available to me.
On the road to our trailer, workers spent several weeks
grading the surface to prepare for mud season.
I worked that fall at a hospital for injured birds,
weighing their small bodies, feeding them mealworms
and berries with my forceps, sometimes using a splint
to repair the hollow bones that make up their wings.

Where am I meant to raise you?
I am waiting for your eyesight to come,
I want to show you the bright orange salamanders we call Red Efts.

II

A NEW NEW ENGLAND

In the children's story, a spider
nested in the young woman's cheek.
Always I would turn to that page purposely.

It is dark and a long drive home.
I tell you again
how I didn't like the movie as a whole,
but I enjoyed it when he climbed inside
the body of a dead horse for warmth.

Out the window, on the wire, the globed silhouette of a guinea fowl.
We count on the poultry to peck through the grass between graves.
We have scattered praying mantis eggs over the field
with the hope that they will hatch to come out and do the same,
devouring the deer ticks who linger, voracious, on the tips of the grass blades.

This evening I am lucid. It lasted two and a half hours,
a film about a man who everyone thought
had died, but in private he went on living.

In private, I go on living,
thinking how later I will miss the country.
The way the brook becomes a river
after long enough rains. Falling asleep some nights
to a high-pitched dying alongside the drone
of the water rushing. Early this morning, I used a hand hoe
to prod gently the thing I had seen in the turned soil
of the autumn vegetable bed. Still pulsing.
I find myself hiding again
and considering the cruelty. How nature
seems terrible, but it's the only thing.
In the afternoons it finally starts cooling.
Soon I will admit that I am here.
I'm turning the pages again, looking to find her.
Rain, like person after person stepping down the stairs of a city bus.

SIRENS

I had two legs and two arms and could fake being
Dog if I used them all four in a crawl.
Sometimes I drank water like this from a bowl on the floor.
Outside, the weather had touched me.
The houses had winked with their lamp eyes.
The ambulances had forgotten to paint their rear windows.
I was an abstract memory of an animal. I wrestled myself
To try and not look inside whenever a new one sirened by.
Sometimes I drank water like this from a bowl on the floor.
I was an animal and in another geological era I was the lines on its palms.
I carried my babies in my mouth by the loose skin on their necks.
I carried my babies, which were fossils.
I carried my babies, who were white-haired.
I put my tongue in the water over and over.
Who were dying.
I carried my babies, who were nothing like me.

FIELD OF VISION

Hunters would venture toward residue and signs.

Fresh scat of buck.

Rhododendron, rub lines, and tracks in the dirt.

Walled in by mountains, primed to something sweet.

The missing person in a face.

I see shapes in the distance, four-legged and running.

The seabirds would stand on the wet rocks and dry out their wings.

A lover of porches.

Modest cities whose whole expanses you can see from the freeway.

Sun on the smaller houses with roofs made from corrugated tin.

I rinse myself.

Only goalposts and roses from here on out.

The bleached, knotted hide for the dog to gnaw.

The seventies wallpaper lining the empty drawer.

No one would see the whole city growing inside.

Alive beside a swing set.

I could see the drugs in my lover's skin and eyes.

I watched the dog busy himself for a whole hour like that.

The coyotes sounded from beyond the trees but were seldom seen.

They shone a light on the breaker box when the house went dark.

We had so much in common I felt.

Seeing how he wetted it down to prepare it for his teeth.

What lives in you fluctuating.

With a metal comb, I would untangle his hair.

I was in trouble for years so kept driving.

What happened to my eyes lately, I could see the way they framed things.

Circular and partially hidden, and everything named.

THE ROOKERY

Herons practice stillness
by the river's worst runoff.
Toxic slough, I see the heads
of rats glide over the surface
of the water: wet fur, they float
toward the river's mouth
with their teeth out, until
love explains itself to me.
By a plank of driftwood,
two heads spin to converge.
Did I never turn over
to touch you. Somewhere
on a Norwegian island,
they are saving the air
in small containers
along with the seeds.
Once you and I lived separately
with a mother and father.
I send the breath
back into my body.
Some evenings
I still find you, playing
a small electric organ
in our bedroom.
The legs of the herons
stay frozen, as the fish
make a ripple. The herons
hold their beaks. In small
containers, they save us
touching. The water's surface
shines with pollution.
I loved you like this,
iridescent, low-level poison.
Like a swimmer dressed in silver,
long-finned, I turn over.
The beak strikes the water.

HULLS COVE

I imagined all the birds alive inside of the place
    only upon hearing the name:
Mount Desert Island. Like an eaten face. Falling
into the part of the water where waves break.

The feminized *a* at the end of a name,
    the way a leaf moves, unagitated
but indisputably circling. It rained.

Having gone with him, soon
enough I was there, living in vain
with the lobsters, red and unseen,
between the mugwort
  and cemetery.

People put it in their mouths
to keep going. Water,
        water, water,

  how much else rhymes with this—

I watched it constitute
     the stream. I loved him.

Strange pronunciation of a word like *solder*.

I loved to give up my life like that.

  Moving water when it's cold, which is nearly always.

MOTEL

I still picture him, sanding the office porch.
We had been working since early spring. The black flies.
A killdeer perched over her single egg in the soil,
squawking periodically. Then the kestrels and saw-whets,
their splayed wings seldom seen through the fog,
shins often banded with small metal rings.
Nevertheless, how they managed to fly freely.

I could recount the pain out loud,
but no one would ever ask this of me.
That mollusk scent. Pushing my cart door to door,
using a lint roller to gather loose hairs from fleece
blankets, swapping and laundering only the sheets.

I watched him shake hands with the guests
as they gave back their keys. A sweet smell
excreted from every shower grate and sink: what persisted,
harmful and cloying, of the offseason's antifreeze.

I knew our neighbor would shoot both horses
as soon as I'd heard that the one of them had lost all its teeth.
I did not expect him to leave their bodies so long in the yard,
plainly visible from the parking lot. Two Clydesdales. Hulking,
uncovered velvet, at long last asleep.

When we fought, I took advantage of our only vacancy,
wrestling loose my own careful hospital corners
to thaw my cold feet. Plentiful yarrow all season,
the lupine beginning as green spread hands, later to climax
with bright purple flowers, rising in cones almost comically.
Abandoned boatyards with ships named for fathers.
Out of Control. Daddy Love. S.S. Glory.

That whole year, an abundance of water.

My soft arms and indecision.

Using a hand mirror to study my backside
for bull's-eyes. Pulling the ticks
from the under-sunned portions of my body.

Why do some people ruin their own lives willfully?

We would undo each trellis
before the first frost, what had once
been beans, tenacious and climbing.
If the one without his teeth were to die
of starvation, then his elderly companion
would soon die, too, out of grief.
I understood, I felt, everything.
I gathered the twine and shook loose
what was left of the dried-out pods
to be buried in time by the snow.

DRIVEWAY

In the gut,
In the mouth,
In the irreducible
    "Bile" humor,
In the middle
    Of the melancholic rainbow,
The green best friend,
The meat seen, in the
Throw-up, pink,
In the irreducible mouth,
In the phrase *didn't like*,
In the outstretched palm
Beside the bull's head,
In the disposable razor's
    Singular softness,
In the overstayed shower,
In the overstayed sober, weak
With few walks and perpetually
    Fogged windows,
In the salty food,
In the heartburn disguising
    The heartache in the
Eventual mouth,
    In the evidential upchuck
        Of the beautiful best friend,
In the last hour,
In the medicine one shan't
        Have taken,
    In the pigeon ooze,
In the cradle of straw
    The crow curves upon,
In the ride to town,
In the unlevel graveyard ground,
In the fire
In the dream

About the people
Lighting themselves
On fire,
On lightning, and lack
Of memory,
In the right way,
The soft light,
The voltage, the numeral,
The hand traced to look
Like a turkey,
In the poor posture,
And the sad mood to prove it,
In the best friend,
In the driveway,
Where caterpillars
Flee tires,
Where the earth shakes
To warn them,
In the ride back from town,
In the medical marijuana,
In the grass-fed butter,
Bring the soul back bring the
Soul back bring the soul
Back bring the soul back, she said.

III

MIRROR LAKE

It trades everything for itself, skin
    of a snake, the manufacture of glass.

Toothless, and loving to hold any thing
in a small-fingered fist,

I arrived on account of nothing—
words being worth less than houses.

DESERT SONNET WITH DROPPED LINE

What you thought was sand but revealed itself to be rock and coarse
shrubbery. You missed Ohio's understated hills. Someone's pores
that made the face feel more accessible by their plain visibility.
A breathing house. Whatever person lives inside of it now

eats and sleeps with or without ease. Unclaimed bicycles sawed
from iron stands at the season's last snowmelt. Again you find yourself lost
in a cream-white nightgown walking the unpaved driveway, sky agate blue.
Most ghosts are female and vaguely resemble you. Bare but for the chia

and piñon pine. You think on the inchworm's maneuvering, to find
yourself in a place unlike the place you started, just by expanding
and contracting in turn against the bark of a tree. You expand.
You contract. The chia. The piñon pine. Her one lax hand

turning the steering wheel on a road of snow. I miss what I almost had.

IT FILLS THE ROOM

I call it *animal* and comb
its brown fur. With tiny beads,
like a toy, for its eyes.
The animal must hunch
to keep its head
from hitting the ceiling. The animal
is this high, this wide—

it fills the room. And I
am there, in the corner,
on a folding chair beside the animal.
See the water bowl by the closed door. I am still
using a flat, round brush to unwork its damp hair.

I have been there a long time. I see myself
from outside. I see the animal
in its small black eyes. I am
with the voice, which says, "Why are you keeping it?"

"Why do you keep it?"

STABLE HAND

How many dreams I had had
of being a boy named Sebastian, big-shouldered
and better off. I would wipe from the floor,

touched by poems about horses. The sky, the banner,
the mountain laurel in some stretches of the South
with hooves and brass ovens, something sounded in there
like this ongoing falling, fistfuls of sand through a stranger's

long digits. I loved to visit the trails outside of town
with you, another gymnasium: in this one the winter sounds,
they sound like nothing. A mask the river wears.
An embarrassing echo of sand. But then always there is

our house full of feathers. The inside-out fowl
where I spend long hours indoors. I love waking and seeing
the half-moon rise from the window's reluctant eye.
I am a stolen child, wearing my new age

like an engagement ring. Believing in the silver that follows
a frozen rainfall, and loving how we live together, in a town

whose bent roads scissor through pastures of dark forms
and now and then horses.

AFTERBIRTH

The small valley, once again filling with rabbits.
I dig through the chamomile fiber, ready for spring,
find in the soil a shard of glass from the jar
I drank out of all last summer, with you
in my stomach, turning.

I remember very little from years prior: the drum
of the underbuilt world, the Tyvek wrap
over the north wall, and loose insulation
like pink cotton candy in the wind.

I keep mixing up my tenses.

Again I lift you over the electric fence
to touch the faces of the cows.
Your whorled hair and eyes of a doll.

This was an owl year but it had been
a mouse year the summer prior.

"Have you ever held the hand of a person as she died?"

We walk through the wealthier sections of town,
admiring the lupines, the roses and statuary, envious
not of the money but the time.

"Yes," I say, "but only figuratively," refusing
the morphine button each occasion it was offered to me.

Sometimes I could tell I was tired by the tremor
in my eyelid. I remember the snake year,
though I've mixed up the seasons.
How there was nowhere to pitch a tent.
They go swift across dirt roads, but slow
to the ascent of our footprints. I have been told

it is dangerous to see your own likeness
from the outside in a dream. Frightened
by their forked tongues and abandoned skin,
I was vigilant the night that I walked out to find her.

Hopeless against the abundant roots of the little white flowers.
Leave them to grow, then.
The whole yard fills with their fragrance as we watch her
mercilessly pulling. In the last few moments before morning,
I approach her from the reeds.
"Enough now," I say, taking hold
of her wet hand.

BRIDGE

It began with a break, an unreachable distance.
Guided by faraway train horns, we rose first
from cracked earth like seedlings in spring. We forgot what had been

and we set about sagging. Ignored how the clouds had shed tendrils
of light, like strings teased from cotton sedge all across our skin.
We grew old and thin. But, sky, I am coming—one hand on the door,
one warming its palm on the dog's sunned fur. Half past twelve

and the flowers are already closing their faces, blind-drunk
on bees' breath and sun. Here is my rent check and sentience. Just the price
for a piece of the doorbell. To cross the bridge you rise first from the dish
where the buildings and traffic lights heap. Overhear a piano. A distant galaxy

keeps dripping: out of tune, it reminds you. We can get back, undressed
by the crass hand of sky. Someone is going to make it out of this dream alive.

IV

RESIDUE

When the sky is pink
and the moon is visible,
and bucks have just sloughed
the last velvet clean off their antlers,
   a new stench of wet
comes unloosed from the trees.

See the bowed turkey vultures, grounded
   in tall grass? I, too, wish to cover
      my whole self in wings.

The ragweed is crowding the old curbside sofas.

The state hospital cemetery
      is still left unlabeled,
an open pasture encircled by trees.

Today it's a field for exercising dogs.

      A knowledge of something beneath.

To sleep again through the whole crowded dream: the alpine lake.
A woman lain across an antique gurney.
      A kitchen fire called Coney Island. Jacob using
a rock for a pillow, waiting for angels, here in the dark
      where a ladder might grow free from anything.

Unharvested stars shed from flags,
      the velvet that's smuggled cold into a poem,
Orion's warped bow.

The antlers that grow back next spring.
      The deer stay alert as they feed on the trees.

My mother asleep on the long boat from Germany.

FINALE OF SEEM

The ice cream truck, slow again tonight
and languorous through the corridor of palms
whose beards quiver high above telephone
          lines. The truck with a whole
room inside it, lit up and selling
          sweet things.

Above the new street, an apron unfolded
and spread over sky. The bats are beginning
          their rounds, fly-thirsty
       and blind. The truck
with the whole room inside it, lit up
and swelling. Hard heath and strawberry cream.
How we all have our humanly hearts
and animal bowels. Towing its room
          down the road. *Do your ears hang low?*
The truck with the whole song
       outside of it. *Do they wobble*
to and fro? I resented its racket, my handwriting
suffered from fever. I shut up in favor
of sounds from the river, and the guardian woodpeckers
again and again at their pockmarked trees.

THERMALS

The lake is not a lake.

I look to find it, my hand
on myself like anything stolen.

But there is no water.

Come nighttime, like poppies
we die back into ourselves.
All evening I do, with my hand
in the shallow.

In the mornings, we water
    the plants. It is this
that they love, what we take
from the river. The burnt hill
we had called California.

All year I was asleep
    inside the long face
of a shoe, loving the past.

No one around and the deer
    still take cover. My hand
on myself reenacting the danger.

Sandhills fly south and we say
how the earthquake will elbow
these houses from sleep.

    Aloft in loose funnels, the eagles
swipe fish from the ospreys'
    loose beaks.

Will I be undressed when it hits,
clipping my toenails over the yellow can?

Aloft in loose funnels, I see eagles. A cliff I drew on.
The bay where the water gets much stiller.

I see my face in the photographs,
smaller than a moth.

Many rocks in these parts are the spit-up of volcanoes.

In the photos we fill our hands with small fossils.
It is this that we love. But there is no water.

All year, how the gulls wrestle otters
for the innards of a clam.

Sometimes they swoop to take the bread right from our hands.

I see smoke around the bend.

But there is no—

no rushing and virile and rhyming
with *daughter*. How it carries the roe
as it courses the land. I love

how I would stand by raining, with my feet weighted down
    like hooves in the sand.

Thieves, when you are ready,
we will all be here waiting
with our hands.

YUCCA VALLEY

What hides in itself in the desert?

I know that I will soon.

Jackrabbits freeze on the gray rocks.

I conjure their faces like long-drawn crucifixions. Juniper
in my pocket. The sage drying blue. I find myself
driving the sand roads and eating for two.

Of course I loved you. Leftover heat
    on a horse's long torso, I go on
palming the sweat where a saddle was. In the dream,
they said I could choose any year to live in.

I packed my clothes into black garbage bags.

I wore my car like a coat and kept moving.

Sand is soft, and a cypress will shoot up from it.
Wind carries perfume from parking lots.

How long did I swing my arm into the dream,
curling my fingers to spoon like a ladle.
There were low-flying bats in there.
The embarrassed, slow-waving frond of a palm.
There was a murder smell but also the soft smell
of bakeries and a village in the hills.
Couldn't have ever been swimming in my life,
        but still, there I was for a good long time
astride over a current in the Salton Sea, in one good place
scarcely moving. Nobody wants to become the small room
          where they've been spending most their time living,
but there are rivers in there.

BEFORE THE BIG AFTERNOON ONCE AGAIN BEGINS

Here is the part of the day when you haven't begun
to consider moving, or starting again. Squirrels
have made a racetrack of the side yard.

You know the sad music that will turn on you
when, spoon to soup, the claws of noon
encroach. Say what has happened to my metaphor.

Say all rise for the verdict.

Say earth eat my blue thing, and mean
something like spasm or ego. Sad ships everywhere.
On this one, two lovers let an unshaved hitchhiker
by the river on board, but they don't know he has a pretty
knife. I saw a movie where two dogs shared

spaghetti. It was perfect. I don't have to tell you, you
saw it, too.

YOU ARE SUPPOSED TO BE FASTENED

Old animal that begs to bloom in the dark,
your paw pads are hard as stone.

Old animal, use your teeth like a comb—try
to avoid the skin as you sift through your fur for mites.

Something about my heart—you are supposed to be
fastened to it, old animal.

Something to do with my desire. You should be
chained to it, and dying.

Old face—I mean this time my own.
They say every five years or so you'll notice,
all at once, that you look entirely different.
Call a spade a spade, and I only get to see it at night.
Old animal, you are my witness. And I'm
trained forever to be on the precipice of change.

Mummies stay warm wrapped in fragments
of Sappho's delectable odes. Never again to fold
from responsibility of face.

Old animal, something about my heart.
Something about your teeth,
or a hairbrush.
Some lack of answers. But who is it who asks?

Tonight the impossible thought in the dark is—

V

PHOENIX RESERVOIR

Loving the dry dust
like sparrows and juncos.
Wing strokes. Impressions
in dirt. I become soft
in the hours of exhaustion,
turning a pebble on the bottom shelf
beside the zinc pills, calling this summer
and loving the scent of our son's wet head.
No longer a student of pain, I had said.

Sometimes I dream I am unmarried again,
watching figures by the man-made lake.
The conceit of a fishing pole, just
some reason to be there alone
in the sun and waiting.

Never too long before waking. That light show
that streams through the window sash.
I see us tear into the dawn like that, making shapes
toward the shadow of his hand with my own.

Weeks amassing like blades
and shrubs into thicket.
I lean into thick heat.
Have me, I think. How the stalks seem
to lick themselves, soil to tip in slow flames.

I was always moving toward something.
Still waters and small streams
where mosquitoes breed. All those deer
in the distance, severed by thicket,
cross-sectioned to reveal only heads.
I see their antlers come up over the foliage again.

And here we are, shaping a path through the rushes,
we are making believe every broad fallen tree is a train.

I now understand, I had meant to love like this always.
I go away, and he remains.

NAMESAKE

Fresh afterthought hurtling through quilted hills,
you are horselike, toward me. All the things
a person should have said. I come from a long line
of harnessed impulses.

Grandfather, when you fall down
from the sky in my dream, you catch
on stray branches and crash
into passenger planes on the way,
and it is all I can do to try and save you.

I mistake for a wound the eagle tattoo
that you got as a sailor, which has turned
        half a century later to nothing,
        bird to puddle, gray gone grayer.

The clouds have left little filaments of white,
        flecked all across your skin. You have grown old and thin.

All along, we thought clouds were just water
    and fog. I drew so close to you,
Grandfather, right after your fall,
now I don't need my winter coat at all.

On visits, you repeat worn-out wisdom and stories. You say horses
will run into stables aflame. Try and usher them out, they about-face
and canter back in toward lit corners, legs already looking, in motion,
like tinder. Hindquarters grown warmer, hooves melting and losing
their shoes. You say they are stupid, Grandfather, how
I look up to you. You feed suet
        to crows, say they recognize faces,
        likewise burning and dangerous places, that horses
are heavenly, but crows are much smarter. Every month
        you are thinner.

In the dream I learn what it means to enter a place that never ends
and is called *age*. I dig into hard earth in pursuit of an abacus.

At night, I barely need a blanket at all.

Still, bandages are useful
so as to swaddle you, Grandpa. It occurs to me, I've never
actually spoken to you. A navy emblem is folding its wings
into a puddle.

Goodbye, eagle.

When you cartwheeled
down from the sky in my dream,
you landed upon a thin latticework of green
which hinted at carrots grown fuller,
more orange, underneath. In the distance, shy rows
of horses hooked tails in the corn, their long faces
tilted in-line toward the silo, their flanks
thick and worn. You are ailing, Grandfather,
and someone is always just out of sight, standing by
to intervene. You wear a thin lanyard necklace
with a little button
to press if you need them.

PARTIALS

Because she had loved the cat so much, it appeared to her
    over and over, taking on different form in dreams. Here she is,

finding it where she mistakenly left it last week,
    carrying it through the city. Careful, she keeps it

from struggling. Collects the mouth, unhinges her jaw in order
  to sing. Promise, there is a river of fish and plenty of mice to eat. I have honored

its occasional claws. Alive in the same clothes for thirty-nine long years,
    near to a century, this thing inside of me.

THE LOONS

I.

To be let out of the house
that is leaking.

The cold of piano keys.

To call across the void to my sister,
whose thin ankle bracelets
make clicks in the breeze.
To call across the space and say,
In the vat dream, the vat
was half full, not half empty.

You had my niece,
who would bob on the surface
like an ocean eider,
unflinchingly.

Now it is my own child's sleeping
radiance that lately compels me.
Quiet hours when I watch his chest
to check for signs of breathing.
Beyond the guttural squall
of discomfort, and
the voiced disturbance
of newly forming teeth.
The quiet hours
when I can see him truly.

II.

At the pond where the tourists
walk wooden planks to preserve

the wetland's ecology,
I saw the loon mother
along with her littles.
She would surface
every five or so minutes
to feed.

These birds were watched
by many others
every evening.

My station rock.
That a cold comes through it.
That the air is thick
and the voice won't carry
without the fluvial
and variable
tremolo, also known
as the "crazy laugh,"
the wail, a wolf comes
bounding through her
beak.

III.

Slow-moving,
desolate mother,
how no mouth
can hold it, no hand
can reach through to it.
Her shadow skewed over
the water, unquilted.
What I want for you
I had wanted once
for myself,
incomprehensible other,
let down by the grease

left on public park
parallel bars,
trying to find
a voice that will suffice
to wake myself fully, only
stifled once more
by the familiar hand
in an ancient dream, I see her
on a crowded ship disembarking
for a brand-new country,
she is tugging softly
at the Coney Island sea kelp
flung over the boardwalk, silent child,
she is walking from the movie
theater once again to the beach.
I would call to her, but I know
it is not for lack of my own
waking voice that
she cannot hear me.

JUNIPER-APPLE RUST

In Omsk, you can find a statue of Dostoevsky.
He looks to be walking on a thin ledge, a balance beam.
As a child, the author once saw a mare whipped by a courtier
and could never forgive the scene. Horses get beaten in most
of his novels and stories, one way or another, alternately over the back
and across the eyes.

You can take the Trans-Siberian Railway from Moscow to the East Sea
and not change one bit. Out your window see skulls, gutted roadkill
that nobody bothers to clean. See the color of rust, home.
The color of snow, nothing.

You can take the Trans-Siberian Railway from Moscow to the East Sea
and not learn anything, and never change your mind. A person gets tired
of moving like that, a person gets tired of her skin.

MEDICINE

In last night's sleeping earth we all had tiny umbrellas,
just enough to shield the crowns of our heads and not
much else. I remember looking at my friend,
with her small, pathetic umbrella. Her wet,
pathetic shoulders catching all that rain. The rain
was coming down hard. No one seemed to think twice
about the unorthodox tininess of our umbrellas.
It seemed we inhabited a world where this was the size
an umbrella was and always had been. I plodded
through puddles, followed family and friends,
reluctantly, down city streets. And then you came by,
bringing a stringed tarantula up toward your wrist,
then letting it fall again toward your shins, and then up
and then down, again, like a yo-yo. You pulled peanuts
from your jeans pocket and shelled them in your
teeth. The rain let up, and you, who held
no umbrella, let fall your poncho. All around me,
people pulled their umbrellas into compact pellets,
and they tucked them into knapsacks and purses.
And then all around me, they took their medicines,
passing around plastic bottles of water with photographs
of glaciers on their labels. Something very far away
was immovable, crystal, and melting. Something
was very beautiful, but we couldn't figure the words for it. You
had no pills with you. Again you resorted to imagining
the perfect beating heart of your Italian grandfather.
Some of us, in the dream, still had memories.

ICHNOFOSSIL

I come home with a string of names
and waterproof place mats. Out the window,
the world appears—granular, slow to focus
and slightly narcoleptic, the cows hide
their faces in one another's fur.

Little ferns unwind into full green fronds.
That oblong shape the lake takes. An overhung branch
where the orb-spider spins her fresh filaments. To think,
how I, too, have grown you out of nothing, almost
thoughtlessly.

I keep rereading the same yellowed page: a small boy
carries a bovine skull in his arms as he runs at low tide
over sand. I want the past back, but with you
somewhere inside of it. In those days, I devoted myself
to rattling old flowers and saving their seeds.

Now the red-haired fox paws her meat in the meadow,
while I make peace with my diminishing narcissism.
Was reality smaller or bigger before you got here? I was
so much like a spider, many-eyed with my coffer of eggs.

Something ruptures the earth and its mark endures.
Again I read you the story where the curious monkey mistakenly
uncovers an uncharted dinosaur bone at a dig. He dislodges dirt
as he trips and falls down the side of a cliff. It has nothing to do
with curiosity, and all the paleontologists come running.

I want the glamour of a scientist who only studies traces
left behind by motion—burrows, trails, and footprints.
Small impressions and gaps between strata of stone.
Your love of fire trucks. My fear of emergency.

Though you are here in the wagon,
I still feel a heel through my stomach's taut skin,
slow and rhythmic in its kicking.

UNDER THE WEATHER

after Hokusai's Under the Wave off Kanagawa

I.

Something comes out of somebody's mouth
in a bad dream and it will not stop. We have crossed
our oars against it. Followed by questions: Is it viscous?
Solid? Liquid, like a stream? At what angle does the spirit
          tilt her skull?

But mother we are moving, and see how the arms
begin to demonstrate age: strong enough now
to lift up and carry the suitcase of light.

We are moving and the mountain is close beside.
Snow-topped, straightened. Something comes out
of somebody's mouth in a dream.

II.

My body like a pupa, bent over the long boat's edge,
holding against the washing, something like that could be
          called daughter.
That was from the mouth: *Pupa*, it had said.

Daughter, nothing but the gradual degradation of the wood blocks used
to stamp out the color and a thick sip to wash down the Dramamine.

III.

The cut fish far away offshore, discarded and silver
in the bath of midnight. How we've likened it to water
for years: the moonlight, a thing you could bathe inside of.

From one cocoon to another I say it: watch me
changing, bent over this boat frame against what comes
from her mouth, slow and thrown up in the dream
of earthquakes and harsh climes, we are treading.

I say I started this world alone, but I started this world inside

IV.

someone. Mother, the vast state of expansion that spills from the mouth
of the child in the dream. Mother, the orchard by morning—where
did those creatures come from to feed? Farmers had tried
at all different methods to frighten off magpies and waxwings.

Is it viscous? The clamor of cockles that make it to shore smelling
of rot and of vagrancy.

A state expands outward, begins to fill the eye socket, starting
from its center. Where did you live? Amniotic, I lived
in the movement. I live here. It consumes me.

I live in the blurry upside-down line of the trees
beneath the line of trees. When you wade
toward a feature its image starts to change.
I shared in their water up to my shins but knew
all the while they were somewhere else completely.

A state expands outward. We can leave this city. I exist
on the surface of the water, but, heaven knows,
I live somewhere else altogether, completely. A country road
where all things and their reflections according to memory meet.

Where one of the beds in the house is a boat. And sand sharks
drift over the carpet in colonies.

V.

Mother a skiff moves silent in the room adjacent you.

Mother we shucked ears of corn.

Mother an eye for your sadness.

Mother a ripple.

Mother the crabs in a line.

Mother the egg-like sunrise.

Mother brought me here in the beginning where else could I have found you.

Mother men forward with sweat and tactless leaning.

Mother the string cheese packed in small sacks.

They propagate lions to take down the deer who host ticks and disease.

Mother I am called one name and not the other one, please.

Mother daybreak.

Mother motion and time.

Mother what feeds the ocean besides a river.

Mother a river.

SO THAT IS WHAT I AM

The way dead people are when they show up, alive, in dreams.
Something is off, most often in their faces. Their expressions
might lack some dimensions. One eye seems swollen, or fixed
to aim right, rapt with something outside of the frame. They
linger in hallways and kitchens; they tempt their survivors
to look at and embrace them. There are marks sometimes
on the backs of their hands, often shining.

"It's just my skin," they all say, but the amorous fleas
soon gather on their forearms to feast. Someone
has collected their hearts in an old scrapyard.
They don't even know they're gone.

ACKNOWLEDGMENTS

These pages are written in solidarity with the people of Palestine and all people resisting empire.

Gratitude to these journals for publishing the following poems, sometimes in earlier forms:

32 Poems: "Bridge" & "The Rookery"

Bennington Review: "Sirens"

Denver Quarterly: "The Rescue"

Gulf Coast: "Desert Sonnet with Dropped Line"

New Ohio Review: "Medicine" & "So That Is What I Am"

Poetry Northwest: "Road Atlas" (published as "Atlas")

Prairie Schooner: "Field of Vision" & "Thermals"

Salamander: "Yucca Valley"

Salt Hill: "Under the Weather"

The Sewanee Review: "Ichnofossil"

Thank you:

to Elisa Gonzalez for seeing something in these poems and selecting this manuscript. My gratitude is immeasurable.

to Louise Glück, whose encouragement brought me back to poetry when

I might otherwise have done something else entirely, and whose wisdom and feedback on an earlier version of this manuscript helped me to see with lucidity what needed to change.

to my first poetry teachers: Ross Gay, Adrian Matejka, and Margaret Ronda. Your influence on my work has been lasting.

to all my fellow poets at the Indiana University MFA—if we ever had workshop together, you can be sure you are a part of this book.

to my dissertation committee at the University of Southern California: Susan McCabe, David St. John, and Mary Sweeney.

to Aracelis Girmay, A. Van Jordan, Patrick Phillips, and L. Lamar Wilson for your eyes and feedback on many of these poems during my time as a Stegner Fellow.

to Catherine Pond, Katie Ogle, and Augustina Evans, for your friendship and vision—without you, this book would not exist.

to Trudie Kaiser, for your imagination, talent, and generosity.

to my beloved circle of eleventh-hour manuscript readers, for your deep attention, insights, and encouragement, which have made this book come together at last: Fatima Jafar, D. M. Spratley, David Hutcheson, Ladan Khoddam-Khorasani, and Dora Prieto.

to the other Stegner Fellows who shared workshop with me, for your ongoing support and incisive feedback on several poems in the collection: Adedayo Agarau, Bhion Achimba, Luci Arbus-Scandiffio, Prairie Moon Dalton, Weijia Pan, Joseph Rios, Bernardo Wade, Dāshaun Washington, and Hua Xi. And to Austen Leah Rose, Essy Stone, Amelia Ada, Victoria Kornick, and Muriel Leung, for your indispensable feedback on the earliest iteration of this manuscript.

to Suzanne, for your unflagging devotion to Vermont pollinators, and for sharing your land, your wisdom, and your love of lupine with me.

to Amy, Annie, Atlanta, Hannah, Lucia, and Maya.

to my parents, endlessly, for your love and generosity, and for encouraging me to do what moves me. Thank you, too, to my sisters, and to Bob and Leslie for your love and support over the years.

Finally, thank you to Jesse and Asa, my truest world—"the light on your door to show that you're home."

NOTES

"Thermals" borrows the following line from T. S. Eliot's *The Waste Land*:

> "But there is no water"

"So That Is What I Am" borrows its title from a line in the poem "Fly" by W. S. Merwin.

GAROUS ABDOLMALEKIAN
Lean Against This Late Hour

PAIGE ACKERSON-KIELY
Dolefully, A Rampart Stands

JOHN ASHBERY
Selected Poems
Self-Portrait in a Convex Mirror

PAUL BEATTY
Joker, Joker, Deuce

JOSHUA BENNETT
Owed
The Sobbing School
The Study of Human Life
We (the People of the United States)

TED BERRIGAN
The Sonnets

LAUREN BERRY
The Lifting Dress

JOE BONOMO
Installations

PHILIP BOOTH
Lifelines: Selected Poems 1950–1999
Selves

JIM CARROLL
Fear of Dreaming: The Selected Poems
Living at the Movies
Void of Course

SU CHO
The Symmetry of Fish

ADRIENNE CHUNG
Organs of Little Importance

RIO CORTEZ
Golden Ax

MARISSA DAVIS
End of Empire

ALISON HAWTHORNE DEMING
Genius Loci
Rope
Stairway to Heaven

CARL DENNIS
Another Reason
Callings
Earthborn
Earthly Virtues
New and Selected Poems 1974–2004
Night School
Practical Gods
Ranking the Wishes
Unknown Friends

DIANE DI PRIMA
Loba

STUART DISCHELL
Backwards Days
Dig Safe

STEPHEN DOBYNS
Velocities: New and Selected Poems 1966–1992

EDWARD DORN
Way More West

HEID E. ERDRICH
Little Big Bully

ROGER FANNING
The Middle Ages

ADAM FOULDS
The Broken Word: An Epic Poem of the British Empire in Kenya, and the Mau Mau Uprising Against It

CARRIE FOUNTAIN
Burn Lake
Instant Winner
The Life

AMY GERSTLER
Dearest Creature
Ghost Girl
Index of Women
Is This My Final Form?
Medicine
Nerve Storm
Scattered at Sea

EUGENE GLORIA
Drivers at the Short-Time Motel
Hoodlum Birds
My Favorite Warlord
Sightseer in This Killing City

DEBORA GREGER
In Darwin's Room

ZEINA HASHEM BECK
O

TERRANCE HAYES
American Sonnets for My Past and Future Assassin
Hip Logic
How to Be Drawn
Lighthead
So to Speak
Wind in a Box

NATHAN HOKS
The Narrow Circle

STEPHANIE HORVATH
Field of Vision

ROBERT HUNTER
Sentinel and Other Poems

MARY KARR
Viper Rum

W. B. KECKLER
Sanskrit of the Body

JACK KEROUAC
Book of Blues
Book of Haikus
Book of Sketches

JOANNA KLINK
Circadian
Days & Chances
Excerpts from a Secret Prophecy
The Nightfields
Raptus

JOANNE KYGER
As Ever: Selected Poems

ANN LAUTERBACH
Door
Hum
If in Time: Selected Poems 1975–2000
On a Stair
Or to Begin Again
Spell
Under the Sign

CORINNE LEE
Plenty
Pyx

PENGUIN POETS

PHILLIS LEVIN
May Day
Mr. Memory & Other Poems

PATRICIA LOCKWOOD
Agate Head / Stone Soup
Motherland Fatherland Homelandsexuals

WILLIAM LOGAN
Rift of Light

J. MICHAEL MARTINEZ
Museum of the Americas
Tarta Americana

ADRIAN MATEJKA
The Big Smoke
Map to the Stars
Mixology
Somebody Else Sold the World

AMBER McBRIDE
Thick with Trouble

MICHAEL McCLURE
Huge Dreams: San Francisco and Beat Poems

ROSE McLARNEY
Colorfast
Forage
Its Day Being Gone

DAVID MELTZER
David's Copy: The Selected Poems of David Meltzer

TERESA K. MILLER
Borderline Fortune

ROBERT MORGAN
Dark Energy
Terroir

CAROL MUSKE-DUKES
Blue Rose
An Octave Above Thunder: New and Selected Poems
Red Trousseau
Twin Cities

ALICE NOTLEY
Being Reflected Upon
Certain Magical Acts
Culture of One
The Descent of Alette
Disobedience
For the Ride
In the Pines
Mysteries of Small Houses

WILLIE PERDOMO
The Crazy Bunch
The Essential Hits of Shorty Bon Bon

DANIEL POPPICK
Fear of Description

LIA PURPURA
It Shouldn't Have Been Beautiful

LAWRENCE RAAB
The History of Forgetting
Visible Signs: New and Selected Poems

BARBARA RAS
The Last Skin
One Hidden Stuff

M.S. REDCHERRIES
mother

MICHAEL ROBBINS
Alien vs. Predator
The Second Sex
Walkman

PATTIANN ROGERS
Flickering
Generations
Holy Heathen Rhapsody
Quickening Fields
Wayfare

SAM SAX
Madness

ROBYN SCHIFF
Information Desk: An Epic
A Woman of Property

WILLIAM STOBB
Absentia
Nervous Systems

MAKSHYA TOLBERT
Shade is a place

TRYFON TOLIDES
An Almost Pure Empty Walking

VINCENT TORO
Hivestruck
Tertulia

PAUL TRAN
All the Flowers Kneeling

SARAH VAP
Viability

ANNE WALDMAN
Gossamurmur
Kill or Cure
Manatee/Humanity
Mesopotopia
Trickster Feminism

JAMES WELCH
Riding the Earthboy 40

PHILIP WHALEN
Overtime: Selected Poems

PHILLIP B. WILLIAMS
Lift Every Voice
Mutiny

MIA S. WILLIS
the space between men

ROBERT WRIGLEY
Anatomy of Melancholy and Other Poems
Beautiful Country
Box
Earthly Meditations: New and Selected Poems
Lives of the Animals
Reign of Snakes
The True Account of Myself as a Bird

MARK YAKICH
The Importance of Peeling Potatoes in Ukraine
Spiritual Exercises
Unrelated Individuals Forming a Group Waiting to Cross